No Exit

Phil Dark

No Exit

No Exit

by

Phil Dark

Adapted form, Huis Clos by - Jean Paul Satre

No Exit

INT.
The large room's decor is exquisite in it's appearance, a large Bronze Ornament adorns the mantelpiece.

A door opens inwards and two voices can be heard talking. A middle aged well groomed man in a blazer, tight-fitted jeans and
smart shoes walks in wide-eyed. RAFAEL is accompanied by a quick witted and bow tied VALET.

RAFAEL
So.
(looking around)
This is it-We're here?

VALET
Yes. Mr Deschanel.

RAFAEL
And this is how it looks?

VALET
Yes.

RAFAEL

I see... Well I guess one must grow accustomed to even the most exquisite furniture-such as these

Second Empire chairs, after a time...I guess.

VALET

Some do. Some don't.

RAFAEL

So are all the others rooms just like this one too?

VALET

What would give you that impression? Sir, we cater for all manner of people here.

(matter of fact)

What would an Asian person for instance want with a Second Empire chair?

RAFAEL

Oh really?! So what use do I have with it?! Do you know who I am?... I mean was..I mean...

(tone change)

It really doesn't matter now, does it?(Pause) If I'm honest, I spent most of my life surrounded by furniture

and people that I didn't much care for. I've even held false positions in boardrooms, companies and governments

whilst still hating everyone I ever met... Some I eventually even grew to like.

VALET

Well you'll find that staying in a Second Empire drawing-room has it's points.

RAFAEL
Really? ..Well I'm sure it does. (taking another look around)
But still I didn't expect anything like this, I mean.. You know what they tell us down there?

VALET
About what?

RAFAEL
Well about.
(sweeping gestures) This-er-residence.

VALET
Now really, sir. Why would you believe such utter nonsense? From people with no such knowledge
and who've clearly never laid foot inside here? Of course if they'd had well..

RAFAEL
Yes, of course..
(Both men begin to laugh Rafael stops abruptly)
But, where are kept? All the thingamajigs, you-know the 'instruments'?

VALET
Excuse me?

RAFAEL
Well, all the torture equipment?

VALET
The, what-now?

RAFAEL
The archaic stuff. You-know hot pokers, whips and what-nots?

VALET
(chuckling)
Oh. Yes of course, "You have jokes" Sir.

RAFAEL
"I have jokes?" But I wasn't... (walking around the room)
I wasn't actually joking. So, no windows or mirrors? Only to be expected and of course nothing breakable...
(His tone changes suddenly)
Would it have killed them to leave me a bloody toothbrush though?!

VALET
Oh that's good sir! Excellent, don't ever let go of that very human dignity and pride-if it pleases you.
...But do excuse my smiling face...

Rafael angrily walks towards the Valet and stops short at an armchair he thumps the armrest heavily.

RAFAEL
I'll ask that you be a bit more respectful to me and yes, I do appreciate the position I'm in-
But you're starting to take the...

VALET
Sir. Please accept my apologies, I meant you no offence. Although, it does get somewhat tiresome.
All our guests always ask the same questions and if I might add silly ones at that. Would you believe the first

question everybody ever asks is 'Where's the torture chamber?'- They're never concerned about hygiene
or their vanities-of that I can assure you. But after a bit, after they have their nerves back so-to-speak.

The Valet's face has a knowing look upon it.

VALET
That's when they begin to pipe up about their toothbrushes, toiletries and what-not. But seriously
Mr Deschanel, use your head. Or perhaps it's better if I'm more direct, what would be the point in you brushing your teeth?

RAFAEL
(Calmer)
Yes, right-of course. Yes of course you're right...

Rafael motions towards the walls.

RAFAEL
Equally why would one want to gaze upon their reflection in a mirror, right?

Rafael then turns to face the Bronze Ornament.

RAFAEL
But this thing over here? That's a whole other story isn't it, I can guess that Bronze thing staring
at me is going to be quite the companion.

He approaches the Bronze ornament on the mantelpiece curiously.

RAFAEL

Yes, I should imagine we'll have many a tournament. Staring each other down-at least until my eyes eventually pop.
(He grins)
Well. It is what it is, I guess...Don't get me wrong, I fully comprehend my position. Bet you'd like to know how it feels?

The dead pan faced Valet doesn't say a word and continues to listen on the off chance of hearing something new.

RAFAEL
Think of a man drowning, losing his breath and choking being suffocated by the water as it inches higher up his body.
Until it's over the man's mouth then nose and only his eyes remain above water... And then,
just as he's about to be swallowed...what does he see? .... A Bronze atrocity by...
(reading from the ornament)
What's the chaps name?-Barbedienne. A collectors piece-none the less.
As in it's a certified Nightmare. (to Valet)
Subtle, their idea I take it...? No, I suppose you're not allowed to answer any of my questions.
I'm not gonna press any further but...I've got a pretty good idea of what I've got coming to me Jeeves,
I'm not the type to get caught off guard...No not me I'm-afraid.
(Dark tone)
I'm fully ready to face this, whatever happens..

He starts to pace around the room.

RAFAEL
(light tone)

So, that's no toothbrush. And no bed, well I guess we never sleep either. Is that so, Jeeves?

VALET
That is so.

RAFAEL
Because of course, why would anyone want to sleep? Utterly useless-like when eyes grow heavy
   and backs of ears tickle-why bother sleep? As drowsiness takes you, simply lie back on the sofa-and
   sleep escapes you. Like the very dreams you chase as you wake it shatters and disappears-then it's gone...
   No sleep, wipe your eyes because it's gone for good and time to start it all over again.

VALET
(Smiling) You're a romantic!

RAFAEL
(Irate)
Don't be so ridiculous!! No I'm not gonna make a scene either, like I said I'll face it-head on like a man.
   I'm saying that I'll not have you springing any surprises on me for your amusement, not before
   I at least get a chance to size it up first..and you call that being romantic?!

The Valet looks on in silence.

RAFAEL
Listen it comes down to this, I don't need to sleep and if I don't feel at all sleepy-why would I care about a bed?

Rafael ponders his own words for a moment.

RAFAEL
No wait, that's not right. In fact- that'd be too easy, no I sense something sinister afoot-Like the notion of life without a rest...

VALET
I don't follow your meaning.

RAFAEL
(questioningly)
You don't follow my meaning?

He eyes the Valet suspiciously.

RAFAEL
I knew there was something off about you, your malevolent gaze violates and there's something
quite beastly about the way you stare. They're paralysed.

VALET
Whatever are you talking about?

RAFAEL
Your eyes, you never blink. Not once, it's unnatural.

VALET
Oh?!

RAFAEL
Did you not know that eyelids are supposed to close-like shutters in a camera? When the eyelids 'blink'

it's takes a split second but it's what happens that's important, a moisture is applied.. A soothing sensation

restful and refreshing blink-blink, four thousand times an hour. You can't imagine just how relaxing it can be...

The Valet face cracks a faint smile.

RAFAEL
So that's it?-You swine! I'm to live without eyelids! It's as plain as day...no eyelids; no sleep, no rest...

My word! But to your twisted games I am wise and as I stated-I am ready to face it, just let me first see it.

Rafael is lively and upbeat he begins to circle the Valet.

RAFAEL
Worry less about my words,
for you see a trickster-I will always be.
I am my own favourite target-my favourite company is me.
I worry less of situations best left to better hands than these...

He stops and faces Valet.

RAFAEL
My thoughts torture me for hours, it's my favourite pastime-perhaps my only real talent.

Down there I did that a lot but I always took breaks to you-know rest.. We had nights to sleep

and days to stress, it was balanced. I wonder what the time is now? Is it daytime or nighttime?

VALET
But Sir,

(sarcastic tone)
Do you not see that the lights are on?

RAFAEL
Bastard! So you're saying that's your idea daytime..? But what of outside?

VALET
(baffled) Out. Side?

RAFAEL
You know what I mean. Past the passage and beyond the wall.

VALET
Oh! Beyond the wall..?

Rafael gives him a look.

VALET
..It's another passage leading to some rooms, stairs and other levels- leading to more passages and more rooms.

RAFAEL
Oh and what lies beyond that?

VALET
That's it.

RAFAEL
Oh really, that's it is it? Surely you're not saying that you work every day? Where do you go on your days off?

VALET

I visit my uncle, he's the Head Valet and has a room on the third floor.

RAFAEL
I should have guessed.

VALET
Anything else?

RAFAEL
Yeah, where's the light switch?

VALET
(Dismissive) There isn't one.

RAFAEL
I can't turn off the lights?

VALET
Well the management can cut the power off to the floor sir, that turns out the lights...
But I don't recall the last time they cut power on this floor if ever. ..We have all the electricity we want.

RAFAEL
You mean I have to live with my eyes open all of the time?!

VALET
(chuckles) 'Live' sir?

RAFAEL
You really are a detestable piece of work, aren't you?-You know what I meant, where is the balance

in perpetual daytime? My eyes ever open...

Rafael paces over to the mantelpiece.

RAFAEL
What about this blasted thing? What if I were to throw it into the lamps? No lamps-no lights...

VALET
It's too heavy for you to move.

RAFAEL
(attempting to move it) Shit! You're right...

VALET
(walking to the door)
Well. Sir, if that is everything I shall take my leave.

RAFAEL
No, don't go just yet..

VALET
(holding the door) Sir..? I have-

RAFAEL
The bell.. Shall I press it when I need you.

VALET
(smiling)
Yes. But it's a sometimes bell-it only works sometimes...

Rafael presses the button there's a faint hum from outside, the Valet looks surprised and tries himself. Again it hums.

VALET
That's unexpected but I really wouldn't rely on it, it's generally faulty.

RAFAEL
But I..

The Valet closes the door on the Rafael. Who begins to pace around the room, picking up a paper knife from the mantelpiece. He presses it against his finger-it's blunt.

He moves to the bronze ornament and looks at it reflectively. He sits down on a chair, then gets up and does a lap of the room ending up back at the mantelpiece. He repeats this several times then approaches the door.

He presses the bell and waits. Nothing.

After a few more seconds he makes a fist and bangs on the door. Nothing. He then beats on it for minutes before he stops and begins to walk away. That's when the door opens and in walks Paula Beddington, followed by the Valet.

VALET
Did you call, Sir?

Rafael stops himself from blurting anything out as his eyes fall upon the voluptuous figured woman. Before answering innocently.

RAFAEL
No.

VALET
Madam. This shall be your room..You must have many questions, everyone has some.
(Paula is silent)
Okay, well if you have any questions about a toothbrush, our lights or that bronze ornament
Mr Deschanel can assist just as well as I. We've already had a little chat, him and I.

Valet exits the room leaving Paula now inspecting the room as Rafael avoids making eye-contact with her. She turns to face Rafael.

PAULA
So where's Jessica?

Rafael is silent.

PAULA
I just asked you a question. Where is she?

RAFAEL
I've got no clue.

PAULA
They wouldn't tell me anything.-You think you're being clever separating her from me like this,
but what you don't realise is that I'm already done with her. Jessica, was a tiresome thing who I won't be missing one bit.

RAFAEL
Excuse me…? What are you talking about? Just who do you think I am?

PAULA
(veiled disgust)
You're the torturer, of course.

Rafael is taken aback then bursts out into laughter.

RAFAEL
I'm your torturer. Do I look like one of the staff to you? You walked in took one look at me and,
well I suppose it's that idiots fault for not introducing us when you first walked in.
My name is Rafael Deschanel. I've held many positions; after starting out as an extensively trained lawyer,
I finished up as a politician with considerable pull. Seeing as we're both in the same boat so-to-speak Mrs..?

PAULA
It's Miss, I've never married.

RAFAEL
Okay. Miss. Well, it's a start I suppose, and now that we've broken the ice... Do I really
look like one of the torturers?-By the way how does one recognise a torturer, clearly you have ideas on the topic.

PAULA
They look... Frightened.

RAFAEL
Frightened?! Of all the...! What in blazes does a torturer have to be frightened of? His victims?

PAULA

Laugh all you want, but I know what I'm talking about.

Rafael stops laughing.

PAULA (CONT'D)
I've often watched myself in the glass.

RAFAEL
(looking around)
In the glass? Damn it, they've removed it all anything resembling it.

There's a short silence before he continues.

RAFAEL
In any case that was a ridiculous statement because I don't look frightened. Don't get me wrong
I do fully appreciate my position and the gravity of the circumstances, I am however ready for whatever comes my way.

PAULA
(shrugs shoulders) That's your own headache.

Rafael is silent.

PAULA
Must you be here all the time or do to take a stroll outside, now and then?

RAFAEL
The door's locked.

PAULA
Oh! ...That is a shame.

RAFAEL
Really. Well I can quite understand how having me here might bore you, I guess that I too would rather
be alone with my thoughts. I need to take stock of my life and put things in order, one does such things
better alone. I'm not such a talkative man, peaceful and easy to live with; I'm sure we'll be able to make it work.
The only thing I would suggest is that we both make a point of being extremely courteous to each other.
This will make it easier on us both.

PAULA
I ain't polite.

RAFAEL
Well then I guess that I will have to be courteous for two.

Rafael sits on a sofa while Paula paces back and forth around the room. She suddenly stops fixated on him.

PAULA
Your mouth!

Rafael sits up startled as if abruptly woken from a dream.

RAFAEL
I beg your pardon.

PAULA
Can't you keep your mouth still? You keep twisting it, it's grotesque.

RAFAEL

I'm so sorry, I wasn't aware of it.

PAULA
That's why I call you out on your bullshit.

Rafael's mouth twitches.

PAULA
There you go! You go on and on about politeness and yet make no attempt whatsoever to control
your face. Remember you're not alone in here; you've no right to inflict me with the sight of your fear.

Rafael gets up and walks over towards her.

RAFAEL
How about you? Aren't you afraid?

PAULA
What's the use? It only made sense before; when we still had hope.

RAFAEL
True there's no more hope-but it's still before. We haven't begun to suffer yet.

PAULA
That so... Well? What's going to happen?

RAFAEL
I don't know yet.

Rafael backs up and then sits back on the couch, while Paula continues to pace back and forth around the room. Rafael's mouth begins to twitch, he glances over towards Paula then puts his head in his hands in silence.

The door quite suddenly begins to open.

In walks a immaculately presented woman of around 30, Claudia Carmella she has a pretty face and a lean skinny body verging on anorexic. She exudes high society pomp and grander and speaks in a manner to match. Accompanied by the Valet.

> CLAUDIA
> (to Rafael)
> Oh, my, gosh-No, please don't look up. I don't even want to see what you're hiding in those hands.

Rafael lifts up his head.

> CLAUDIA
> What? ... I don't even know you...?

> RAFAEL
> I can assure you that I am not your torturer.

> CLAUDIA
> I didn't say you were, I thought someone might be playing a rather nasty trick on me.
> (to the Valet)
> Is anyone else coming?

> VALET
> No madam. No one else is coming.

> CLAUDIA

Is that so? So we're to stay here by ourselves, the lady, this gentleman...(starts laughing) and myself.

RAFAEL
It's not funny.

CLAUDIA
(laughing)
It's these ghastly sofas they're simply hideous to look at and just look at the way they've been arranged,
it's like visiting my boring aunt May, on a New Year's Day! Her house was always full of atrocities like that...
And I suppose each has their own that one is supposed to be mine? (to the Valet)
Oh but you can't expect me to sit on that it'd be too horrific for words, that sofa is vivid green
and my dress as you see is a pale blue.

PAULA
You can have mine. If you'd prefer.

CLAUDIA
Oh that claret coloured one, you mean? That's so sweet of you dear, but really I don't think it'd be so much better.
Oh well, what's the use in worrying anyway I guess? We've got to take what's coming to us, I'll stick with the green.

There's a brief pause.

CLAUDIA
The only one that might do at a pinch...Is the gentleman's...

Paula turns to Rafael who suddenly appears to be in his own thoughts.

> PAULA
> Did you hear that, Mr Deschanel?

> RAFAEL
> Oh–the sofa, you mean?

He stands up.

> RAFAEL
> Please, do take it. Madam.

Claudia takes off her jacket and places it on the sofa.

> CLAUDIA
> Thank you. Well, seeing as we're to live together we might as well introduce ourselves.
> My name is Carmella, Claudia Carmella.

Rafael still standing bows politely. But before he begins his introduction Paula has stepped ahead of him and speaks first.

> PAULA
> Paula Beddington. Very pleased to meet you.

Rafael bows again and introduces himself.

> RAFAEL
> Rafael Deschanel.

> VALET
> Do you require me any longer?

CLAUDIA
No, you can go now. I'll ring when I want you.

The Valet bows politely towards each of them before closing the door behind him.

PAULA
You're so pretty. I wish I had flowers to welcome you.

CLAUDIA
Flowers? Yes I used to love flowers. But they fade so fast and it's so stuffy in here I doubt they'd last very long.
Oh well, I guess the main thing now is to remain cheerful don't you agree? Of course you do,
after all like me you're both already...

PAULA
Yes, last week. How about you?

CLAUDIA
Oh, I'm a new arrival my departure was quite recent... Yesterday. Yes, in fact the service is still ongoing.

Claudia appears to be looking at something, her eyes gaze off into space as she speaks in a flat descriptive tone.

CLAUDIA
My sisters veil keeps being blown off by by the wind. She's trying her very best not to cry,
come my dear surely you can do better than that. That's better, those are real tears your veil. OMG,
Verity looks so sophisticated and smart. She's holding my sister's arm. Verity was one of my best friends,

from childhood like forever.

Claudia is smiling as she speaks.

> PAULA
> Did you suffer much?

> CLAUDIA
> Oh no, I was only half conscious. Mostly.

> PAULA
> How did you?

> CLAUDIA
> Pneumonia.

Her tone reverts back.

> CLAUDIA
> It's over now and they're all leaving the cemetery, goodbyes all around. Quite the turnout.
> Husband stayed out home, tormented and prostrated...poor man.
> (To Paula)
> How about you?

> PAULA
> The gas stove.

> CLAUDIA
> (Incredulous)
> The what now?

Claudia quickly moves on to Rafael before any follow up.

CLAUDIA
How about you?

RAFAEL
Bullet to the head.

CLAUDIA
Oh dear, oh my... Sorry! I'm afraid I'm not great company amongst the dead.

PAULA
Please don't say that word. It's such a crude word and well, it doesn't feel right. I know the situation but
if I'm being honest I don't think I've ever felt as alive as I do now.

Both Rafael and Claudia are silently listening to her words.

PAULA
I've been thinking about that a lot, we need another thing to call ourselves. I think that we should be called 'Absentees'...

She turns to Rafael.

PAULA
So, have you been absent for long?

RAFAEL
About a month.

PAULA
Where are you from?

RAFAEL
I'm from the U.K

CLAUDIA
I'm from Paris. Have you left anyone there?

RAFAEL
Yes, my wife.

Rafael's eyes drift off as he begins to visualise something in front of him. His tone switches to one similar to Claudia's tone during visions.

RAFAEL
She's wearing all black busying herself about the house. She has that same vacant stare she always had, t
hat martyred look never left her face. Oh how it used to drive me insane!

Rafael sits down with his hands over his face, deep in thought.

PAULA
...Claudia...!

CLAUDIA
Please, Mr Deschanel!

RAFAEL
What is it?

CLAUDIA
You're sitting on my sofa.

Rafael gets up.

RAFAEL
I do beg your pardon.

CLAUDIA
You looked so, so far away… I'm sorry I disturbed you.

RAFAEL
Don't mention it. I was just getting my thoughts and my life in order.

Paula bursts out laughing.

RAFAEL
Yes, you may laugh. But you'd do better by following my example.

PAULA
No need. My life's in perfect order. It sorted itself out on it's own accord, so I needn't bother now.

RAFAEL
Really? You imagine it's as simple as that, suppose.

Rafael seems flustered and runs his fingers through his hair.

RAFAEL
My my, the heat in this place. Rafael begins to take off his Jacket…

CLAUDIA
(Incredulous) How dare you?
(softly)
No, please don't. I find men in shirt sleeves simply abhorrent.

RAFAEL
Oh, right. Forgive me my manners. When I was you-know we spent most nights debating with jackets off
sleeves rolled up and a stiff drink.

He puts his jacket on properly.

RAFAEL
Nights down in the barracks-as we used to call it, war rooms and conferences always underground
with the air-con continuously running but still always, stiflingly hot... Stiflingly hot like now, it's ridiculous in here.

He runs his finger around his collar to emphasise.

RAFAEL
It's nighttime now.

CLAUDIA
Evidently so. Verity's undressing; so it must be past midnight. How quickly time flies, on earth that is.

PAULA
Yes. Definitely after midnight. They've sealed up my old room, it's pitch black and empty.

RAFAEL
Oh yes, the boys all have their jackets off and sleeves rolled up... Cigars burn, cognac flows and the air
is thick and musky... I'm growing to miss the the company of my fellow man.

CLAUDIA

>   (aggressive)
>   Well, that's where are tastes differ. Don't know what I thought I'd expect from a politician.

She turns to Paula.

> CLAUDIA
> What about you? Do you like men in shirt-sleeves?

> PAULA
> Oh, I don't care much for men at all. In any way.

Claudia has an air of dominance about her as she looks at the two in puzzlement.

> CLAUDIA
> You know, for the life of me I cannot imagine why they would put the three of us together. It's just…It makes no sense.

Paula stifles a laugh.

> PAULA
> What's that you say?

> CLAUDIA
> This situation, I'm looking at the two of you and thinking how are we supposed to live together…
> One would expect to see old friends, relatives a familiar face.

> PAULA
> Oh yes, a charming old friend-with a whole in the middle of his face.

> CLAUDIA

Yes, that tall dark hardbody from down the road that looks like he knows how to tango.

...But why put the three of us together?

RAFAEL
It's what you might call a fluke, first come first served to be precise. The Valet told me every room is different,
perhaps we're deemed comparable on some variable we've not considered. If you look at things on a macro scale...

He turns agitated to a laughing Paula.

RAFAEL
And what do you find so funny?

PAULA
It's you! You and your stupid flukes. As if they'd leave anything down to chance...
But you can keep telling yourself whatever you want to believe like the stuffy politician that you are.

Rafael cuts her a wicked stare which Paula matches straight back, he then goes back into his thoughts. Claudia hesitantly breaks the silence.

CLAUDIA
I'm beginning to wonder. Do you think it's possible that we've met at some point in our lives?

Paula adjusts herself in her sofa and looks directly into Claudia's eyes.

PAULA
Never. I would never have forgotten you.

CLAUDIA
Maybe there's another connection, we might have friends in common. Do you know the Dubois-Seymours?

PAULA
Not likely.

CLAUDIA
But... Everyone went to their parties.

PAULA
What are their jobs?

CLAUDIA
Oh, they don't do anything. But they have an amazing property out in the country and they host
the most lavish parties. They host people from every corner of the earth.

PAULA
Not me. I'm a gym assistant.

Claudia recoils slightly.

CLAUDIA
Ah, yes... Of course, in that case- and what of you, Mr Deschanel?

RAFAEL
(dismissive)
No we've never met.

CLAUDIA

Then you must be right, it's mere chance that had put us together. A fluke.

Paula has had enough.

PAULA
Mere chance, you say? So is it also by mere chance that the room is decked out like this?
So it's an accident that the sofa on the right is a livid green and the one on the left is wine red?
Mere chance, yeah? Well just try and move those sofas and you'll see the difference quick enough.
Like that monstrosity on the mantelpiece, do you think that's an accident? Then there's the heat.
What about that?

All three are silent for a moment before Paula continues.

PAULA
I tell you they thought it all out. Down to the last detail. Nothing was left to chance. This room was all set up for us.

CLAUDIA
But really! Everything here is so hideous; in all angles, it's so uncomfortable. I've always loathed angles.

PAULA
(shrugging shoulders)
And you think I lived in a second empire drawing room?

CLAUDIA
So it was all fixed up beforehand?

PAULA
Yes. And they've put us together deliberately.

CLAUDIA
Then it's no accident that you are seated precisely opposite me? But what can the idea behind it be?

PAULA
I got nothing. I only know that they're waiting.

CLAUDIA
I see, well I could never bear the idea of being expected to do something-In fact it always made me
want to do the exact opposite.

PAULA
Good on you-you should do it. Do it if you can, but how do you know what they expect?

Claudia stamps her feet.

CLAUDIA
This is outrageous! (eying the other two)
Something is coming to me, from the two of you... Something nasty, I know it. I know faces,
they tell you a lot about a person. Some faces tell me everything at once but yours, don't convey anything.

Rafael turns abruptly to Paula.

RAFAEL
Look here! That's quite enough of this. Why are we together? We've had enough of your little

hints and cheeky comments so you might as well stop beating about the bush and come out with it.

PAULA
But I know nothing absolutely nothing it. I'm as much in the dark as you.

Rafael looks puzzled.

RAFAEL
But we must have answers, we need answers.

PAULA
If only each of us had the balls to tell-

RAFAEL
-To tell what?

PAULA
Oh, touch a nerve? Claudia!

CLAUDIA
Yes?

PAULA
What have you done? ... I mean, why have they sent you here?

CLAUDIA
That's just it. I have no notion as to why I'm here, not the foggiest. In fact I'm now quite sure there's been a ghastly mixup.
(to Paula)
Don't smile. Seriously think about the shear numbers of...'absentees' everyday, all being categorised,

considered and placed. All managed by the dregs and plebs, you know the lowers who-never get a break,
their bound to make mistakes...Don't smile.

She turns to Rafael.

CLAUDIA
Why don't you speak? If they made a mistake in my case, they may have done the same with you.
(to Paula)
And to you... In any case isn't it always better to think that we got here by mistake.

The briefest of silences.

PAULA
Is that all that you have to tell us?

CLAUDIA
Well, what else shall I tell? I have nothings to hide. I lost my parents when I was a child and had to bring up
my younger brother. We were terribly poor and my brother had medical conditions, you understand
so when a wealthy old friend of my family asked me to marry him I said yes. He was nice but many years
my senior-old enough to be my father and although I didn't love him everything was fine, my brother got
the attention needed and we were happy for six years. Then two years ago I met the man I fell in love with,
he asked me to run away with him and I refused. Then a week later I caught pneumonia which finished me off.

She exhales then takes a long deep breath before finishing.

> CLAUDIA
> That's the full story, that's it. Undoubtedly by certain standards I did wrong to sacrifice my youth
>   for a man nearly three times my age.

She turns to Rafael.

> CLAUDIA
> Do you think it's a sin?

> RAFAEL
> Certainly not.

Rafael pauses momentarily before continuing.

> RAFAEL
> And now, tell me, do you think it's a sin to stand by one's principles?

> CLAUDIA
> Of course not. Surely no one could blame a man for that.

> RAFAEL
> Wait a bit! I always put my constituents, my country first our investment portfolio included low cost
>   housing developments, skills training and work placement schemes. Then came the great 2nd Great Depression
>   everyone was losing their jobs, their security, their livelihoods.

He sits up animated almost as if addressing a hall of people instead of the two others in the drawing room.

RAFAEL
Of course everyone looked to me wanting to know how to create, Utopia. I told them once we can straighten
out our own country we will help out other nations. They didn't listen to reasoning but I stuck to my beliefs,
like a man should.

CLAUDIA
I completely agree.

RAFAEL
In their times of need I exemplified success and championed my cause giving financial opportunities
and a platform to the voiceless oppressed.
And when we're being overrun by the savages I stood tall, I did everything in my power to prevent the erasure
of our culture, history and my people. Then I was brutally shot dead a few weeks before the general election,
which I was forecast to win. Was I so wrong?

Claudia rests her hand gently on his arm.

CLAUDIA
Wrong? No. You weren't wrong, on the contrary you were a-

PAULA
-A hero! And how about your wife, Mr Deschanel?

RAFAEL
That's simple, I'd rescued her from the gutter.

Claudia turns to Paula.

CLAUDIA
You see! You see!

PAULA
Yes I see all right...

All three are silent for a moment.

PAULA
Look! What's the point of all the play-acting? All this throwing shit in each other's eyes is meaningless,
we're all here tarred with the same brush.

CLAUDIA
How dare you?!

A faint smile crosses Paula's face for a second before she speaks.

PAULA
Yes, we are criminals-murderers-all three of us. We're in HELL! They don't make mistakes,
and people aren't damned for nothing.

CLAUDIA
Stop. For heaven's sake-

PAULA
In HELL! Damned souls-that's us, all three!

CLAUDIA
Keep quiet! I forbid you to use such disgusting words.

PAULA

A damned soul-that's you, my little plaster saint. And ditto our friend there, the noble politician.

We've had our hour of pleasure haven't we? There have been people who have burned their entire lives out

for our sakes-and we chuckled over it. So now we have to pay the reckoning.

Rafael has had enough and raises a clenched fist towards Paula.

RAFAEL
Will you keep your mouth shut, damn it!

This takes Paula by surprise but she confronts Rafael fearlessly.

PAULA
Well, well! ... I think I understand now. Why they've put the three of us together.

RAFAEL
I'll advise you to-to think carefully before continuing...

PAULA
Wait! Hear me out. This isn't complex, it's simple. Childishly simple.

She has the room's undivided attention.

PAULA
Firstly. We can all agree that there's no physical injury to us, right? But yet, we're in hell.

Rafael wipes his forehead and runs his fingers around his shirt collar.

PAULA

And no one else will come here, ever. We'll stay in this room together, the three of us, forever and ever...

In short someone is absent. The official torturer.

RAFAEL
Yes. Well I'd noticed that too.

PAULA
It's obvious what they're after, an economy of man-power or should I say devil-power.

It's like one of them all you can eat cafes, you get taken to your table then you serve yourselves.

CLAUDIA
What-ever do you mean?

PAULA
I mean that, each of us will act as a torturer for the other.

All three are silent as they digest the words and the implication.

RAFAEL
(Calmly)
No. I shall never be your torturer. I wish neither of you harm, and I've really no concern with you.

None at all. So if that is the case the solution's simple enough; each of us stays put in their own corner
and takes no notice of the others.

Rafael stands up and gestures to the two.

RAFAEL

You there, you there and me here. Also, we mustn't talk to one and other. Silence, not a word.

Like soldiers at their posts so too must we remain, silent and resolute.

That won't be difficult; each one of us has enough material to occupy ourselves with. With just my thoughts alone

as company I could easily sit for ten thousand years.

CLAUDIA
Have 'I' got to keep silent too?

RAFAEL
Yes. And that way we-we'll work out our salvation. Looking into ourselves never raising our heads. Agreed?

He looks over to Paula.

PAULA
Agreed.

He looks back at Claudia who is hesitant.

CLAUDIA
Agreed.

Rafael nods his head.

RAFAEL
Okay then. Good-bye.

He then goes directly to his seat and places his head in his hands.

There is a long silence before it is broken by the sound of Paula singing to herself.

PAULA
(singing)
Oh what a crowd of people that awaits at Pentonville gates,
they've shipped you in but you sealed your fate,
the clocks has stopped your jobs to wait,
they stack you up then ship like crates,
Oh what a crowd of people that awaits at Rikers gates,
they've shipped you in but you sealed your fate,
the clocks have stopped your jobs to wait,
they stack you up then ship like crates,
Oh what a crowd of people that awaits at La Santé gates,
they've shipped you in but you sealed your fate,
the clocks have stopped your jobs to wait-

Meanwhile Claudia who has been plying herself with powder puff and lipstick now twists her head in search of a wall mirror, then fumbles about in her bag before turning to Rafael politely.

CLAUDIA
Excuse me, have you a mirror?

Rafael ignores her.

CLAUDIA
Any type of mirror would do, maybe a pocket one?

Rafael doesn't move a muscle.

CLAUDIA
Even if you won't speak to me, you could still lend me a mirror.

Paula smiles briefly to herself.

> PAULA
> Don't worry, I've got a mirror. You can borrow mine.

Paula starts rummaging through her own bag.

> PAULA
> (angrily)
> It's gone! They must have taken it off me at the entrance.

> CLAUDIA
> (Standing up)
> How bloody tiresome!!

She stands with her eyes shut and silent. Slowly she starts to sway from side to side as if to faint. Paula rushes up from her chair to catch her in time, holding her in her arms.

> PAULA
> What's the matter?

Claudia opens her eyes slowly and smiles.

> CLAUDIA
> Oh my, I feel so queer. Claudia pats herself on her chest.

> CLAUDIA
> Do you ever get taken that way? When I can't see myself I start to panic,
> I begin to wonder if I really truly exist. I pat myself to make sure, doesn't help though.

PAULA
You're lucky. I'm always conscious of myself-in my mind. Painfully so.

CLAUDIA
Ah yes, in your mind. But everything that goes on in one's head is all very vague isn't it?
It all just makes you want to go to sleep.

Claudia stands on her own accord and she is silent for a moment.

CLAUDIA
I have six big mirrors in my bedroom. There they are, I can see them. But, they can't see me.

Claudia has that distant look I'm her eyes.

CLAUDIA
They're reflecting the carpet, the settee, the window. But how empty it is a mirror without a reflection.
When I talked to people I used to position myself near mirrors so that I could see my reflection as I spoke,
I always found it comforting seeing myself as others see me. Something about it used to keep me, sharp and alert...
Oh dear! My lipstick! I'm sure I've put it on all crooked.
No, I simply can't do without a mirror for-ever and ever. I just can't.

PAULA
Well, what if I can be your looking glass… Come and pay me a visit dear, there's a space for you
right here on my sofa.

Claudia points to Rafael.

CLAUDIA
But-

PAULA
Oh he doesn't count.

CLAUDIA
But we're going to-to hurt each other. You said it yourself.

Paula doesn't skip a beat.

PAULA
Do I really look like I want to hurt, you?

CLAUDIA
One can never tell.

PAULA
If anything, it's much more likely that you will hurt me. But who cares. If I've got to suffer,
 it may as well be by your hands. Your pretty hands. Come, sit down.

Paula takes Claudia by the hand and leads her to the sofa where they both sit.

PAULA
Come closer, closer to me. Look into my eyes and tell me what you see?

Claudia and Paula are now sitting with their faces an inch apart.

CLAUDIA

I'm there. I can see myself but I'm so little, I can't see myself properly.

PAULA
But I can. Every inch of you... Now, ask me any question. I'll be as candid as any mirror.

Claudia looks slightly embarrassed and looks towards Rafael her eyes appealing for his assistance.

CLAUDIA
Please, Mr Deschanel. Are you sure that our chatter, is not bothering you?

Rafael doesn't move a muscle.

PAULA
Don't worry about him. I told you, he doesn't count. We're alone in here, it's just you and me. Ask away.

CLAUDIA
Are my lips all right?

PAULA
Show me. No, they're a bit smudgy.

CLAUDIA
I thought as much. (glances at Rafael)
It's a good job no one's seen me, I'll try again.

Claudia cleans off the lipstick and begins to reapply carefully.

PAULA

That's better. No, follow the line of your lip. Stop! Look, give me your hand and let me guide you.

Paula gently takes Claudia's hand and guides the application of lipstick.

PAULA
There. That's quite good.

CLAUDIA
As good as when I came in?

PAULA
Far better. Crueler. Your mouth looks diabolical now.

CLAUDIA
Good gracious! And you say you like it! This situation is diabolical to say the least and quite maddening
not being able to see oneself. Look here Ms Beddington, are you sure that it's alright now?

PAULA
Won't you call me Paula?

CLAUDIA
Are you sure it looks all right?

PAULA
You're lovely, Claudia.

CLAUDIA
But how can I rely on your taste? Is it the same as my taste? Oh how sickening this all is, enough to drive one crazy!

PAULA
I have your tastes, my dear, because I like you so much. Look at me.

Paula gently places a hand on her knee.

PAULA
No, straight at me. Now smile. I'm not so ugly, either. Am I not nicer than your mirror?

CLAUDIA
Oh, I don't know. You do scare me so, my reflection never did that to me; but of course I knew it so well.
Like something I had tamed... I'm going to smile, and my smile will sink down into your pupils, and heaven
knows what it'll become.

PAULA
And why shouldn't you "tame" me?

The two women begin to gaze at each other, Claudia in a type of fearful fascination.

PAULA
Listen, I want you to call me Paula. We must be great friends.

CLAUDIA
I don't make friends with women very easily.

PAULA
Not with a working class gym instructor you mean...? Hello! What's that nasty little red spot at
the bottom of your left cheek? A pimple?

CLAUDIA
(gasping)
A pimple?! Oh how foul! Where?

Paula points to Claudia's face.

PAULA
There... You know how they catch the little Lark, birds? With a mirror. I'm your Lark-mirror, my dear, and you can't escape me.

Paula smiles.

PAULA
There isn't any pimple, not a trace of one. But what about it? Suppose the mirror started telling lies?
Or suppose I started covering my eyes- as he's doing-and refused to look at you, all that loveliness of yours
would be wasted in the desert air.

Paula gently strokes a fallen lock of Claudia's hair back into place.

PAULA
No, don't be afraid. I can't help looking at you. I shan't turn my eyes away. And I'll be nice to you,
ever so nice to you. Only you must be nice to me, too.

There's a short silence between the two.

CLAUDIA
Are you really, attracted by me?

PAULA
Very much.

Claudia looks towards Rafael who hasn't moved a muscle.

> CLAUDIA
> But I wish he'd notice me, too.

> PAULA
> Oh course! Cos he's a man!

Paula gets up and walks over to Rafael.

> PAULA
> You've won!

Rafael doesn't say a word.

> PAULA
> But for fucks sake, look at her damn it!

Rafael is still silent as Paula begins to get more agitated getting in his face from different angles.

> PAULA
> Don't pretend. Don't you pretend you missed a word of what we've said.

Rafael lowers his hands and lifts his head.

> RAFAEL
> Quite so; not a word. I stuck my fingers in my ears, but the sound of your voices kept pounding in my brain.
> Silly chatter. I'm not interested in you. Now, will you two leave me in peace?

PAULA
Not in me, perhaps-but how about this child? Aren't you interested in her? Yeah, I saw through
your little game-jumping on your high horse just to impress her

RAFAEL
I asked you to leave me in peace. There's someone talking about me in 'the bunker', and I'm trying to listen
to what they're saying. And if it makes you feel any better, I have no use for the "child" as you call her.

CLAUDIA
Thanks!

RAFAEL
Oh, I didn't mean it rudely.

CLAUDIA
You reprobate bastard!

Both Claudia and Rafael both stand up and square off against each other in an intense silence.

RAFAEL
So that's that then, good... You know I begged you not to speak.

CLAUDIA
It's her fault; she started. I didn't ask anything of her and yet she came and offered me her, her mirror...

PAULA

Yeah, so you say. But you were busy tarting yourself up for him, all the time-trying anything you could to get his attention.

CLAUDIA
Well, why shouldn't I?

Rafael interjects.

RAFAEL
You're crazy, both of you. Don't you see where all this is leading us? This is why I told us not to speak.
So keep your mouths shut!

He takes a moment to compose himself and let the words sink in.

RAFAEL
Now let's go back to our seats calmly and quietly, without saying anything; we'll look at the floor and each
of us must try to forget the others are there.

All three of them stand in silence for a moment, then they all make their ways back to their chairs. Suddenly Paula turns on Rafael in enraged anger!

PAULA
To forget about the others? How utterly absurd! I feel you there, in every pore. Your silence clambers
in my ears like church bells. You can nail your mouth shut and cut out your tongue-but you can't prevent
yourself being there. Can you stop your thoughts? I hear them, ticking away like a clock, tick tock, tick tock,
and I'm sure you can hear mine too.

Rafael and Claudia listen on in silence not knowing how to react to Paula who is clearly not backing down.

PAULA
It's all very well skulking on the sofa, but you're everywhere, and every sound comes to me soiled,
because you've intercepted it on it's way. Why, you've even stolen my face!
I don't even know it anymore but you see it all the time!

Rafael gives a brief look of puzzlement. Paula points towards Claudia.

PAULA
And what about her-what about, Claudia? You've stolen her from me, too; if she and I had been all alone
do you think she'd be treating me like this?

Rafael's heard enough and takes his seat putting his head in his hands.

PAULA
No, take your hands from your face, I won't leave you in peace-that would suit your book all too well.
You'd go on sitting there in a trance, like a yogi, and even if I didn't see her I'd still feel it in my bones-that she
was making every sound, even the rustle of her dress, for your benefit, throwing you smiles you don't see...
Well, I won't stand for that, I prefer to choose my hell; I prefer to look you in the eye and fight it out face to face.

RAFAEL
Have it your way.

Rafael stands up slowly.

RAFAEL
I suppose it was always bound to come to this; they knew what they wanted and we're easy game.
If they'd put me in a room with men- men can keep their mouths shut. But it seems there's no point in wanting the impossible.

He casually walks over to the side of Claudia's chair and then begins to lightly fondle her neck.

RAFAEL
So, I attract you, little girl? It seems you've been making eyes at me.

She brushes his hand away in defiant disgust.

CLAUDIA
Don't touch me.

RAFAEL
Why ever not? We might be, you know, quite natural…

He thinks for a moment.

RAFAEL
Do you know, I used to be mad about women? Some were even fond of me. So, we might as well stop posing,
we've got nothing to lose. Why trouble ourselves with politeness, etiquette and all the rest of it?
We'll soon be as naked as-as newborn babies.

CLAUDIA
Oh let me be!

RAFAEL
As newborn babies. Well, don't say I didn't warn you. I asked so little of you, nothing but peace and silence.
I'd put my fingers in my ears. James was sprouting away as usual, in the centre of the room, with all my peers
listening. In their shirt sleeves. I tried to hear, but it wasn't too easy.
Things on earth move so quickly, you know. Now it's over, he's stopped talking, and what he thinks of me has gone back into his
head. Well, I've got to see it through some-how...

He fades in and out of his distant looks, he gives his eyes a rub.

RAFAEL
Naked as we were born. So much the better; I want to know whom I have to deal with.

PAULA
You already know there's nothing more to learn.

RAFAEL
(dismissive)
You're wrong. And as long as each of us decide against making a clean slate of it- tell why they've been damned-
we know nothing. Nothing that counts.

He faces Claudia.

RAFAEL
You, young lady, will go first. Why? Tell us why. If you're frank, if we bring our hidden spectres
into the open, it may save us from disaster. So-out with it. Why?

Claudia rolls her eyes.

CLAUDIA
I tell you I haven't a notion. They wouldn't tell me why.

RAFAEL
That so? They wouldn't tell me either but I've got a pretty good idea... Perhaps your shy of speaking first?
Right, I'll lead off.

Rafael takes a few moments as he considers his words.

RAFAEL
I wasn't really a friend of my constituents, in fact we often instigated policies that sounded helpful-when sold
to the people, but were tailored to keep them languishing in the despair that we ourselves had manufactured.
Like a farmer with his cattle so too did I monetise the population for my benefit.

PAULA
You were a politician, we already know that.

RAFAEL
Be quiet. And listen as that is but a side-issue.

He takes a brief pause before continuing.

RAFAEL
I'm here because I treated my wife, abominably. That's all.

PAULA
How can you be so certain, if they didn't tell you anything?

Rafael ignores her and she let's him continue speaking.

RAFAEL
For 5 years, I destroyed that woman. Naturally, she's still suffering. There she is:
The moment I mention her, I see her. It's James who interests me, and it's her I see. Where's James got to?

His mind seems to be drifting in and out of something, his eyes dart from left to right as if he is scrolling through searching for something only his eyes see.

RAFAEL
For five years. There! They've given her my possessions back; She's sitting by the window,
with my coat on her knees. The blood soaked coat I was wearing when, when… The blood's like rust.
It's a Luis Farrakargo. Very fancy! It belongs in a museum now, after all; I used to wear that coat!

He pauses and takes a deep breath.

RAFAEL
Now, can't you shed a tear, my love! Surely you can squeeze one out- at last? No? Can't manage it?

Rafael goes over to the fireplace and tries to loosen his neck from his shirt, he looks uncomfortable. He pushes the letter opener to the side and rests with his back against it, all the time deep in thought.

RAFAEL
Night after night I came home blind drunk, stinking of alcohol and women. She always sat up for me, of course.

But she never shed a tear. She never cried, she never criticised, she'd just sit there. Only her eyes ever spoke.

He starts slowly pacing.

RAFAEL
Big, tragic eyes. I don't regret anything. I must pay the price, and I shan't whine... It's snowing in the streets now.
Won't you cry, damn it? That woman was a born martyr, you know; a victim by vocation.

PAULA
(genuine)
Why did you hurt her like that?

Rafael answer immediately.

RAFAEL
It was easy. Just a word was enough to make her flinch. Like a sensitive-flower. She'd never, never criticise me...
I am fond of teasing. I have my tricks, I watched and waited. But no, not a tear, not a protest. I'd picked her up
out the gutter, under-stand...

His still observing something thoughtfully as he speaks.

RAFAEL
Now she's stroking the coat. Her eyes are shut and she's running her fingers over the dry blood.
What are you after? What do you expect? I tell you I regret noth-ing! The truth is, she admired me too much.
Does that mean anything to you?

He looks towards Paula.

> PAULA
> No. Nobody admired me.

> RAFAEL
> So much the better. So much the better for you. Well, I suppose of all this must strike you as rather vague...
> Here's something for you to get your teeth into.

He gives Paula another quick glance.

> RAFAEL
> I've been in favour of and supported segregation my entire political career. But I took in a mixed
> darkie lodger in our house, for re-search purposes... My wife slept upstairs; she must have heard- everything.
> She was an early riser and, as I and the boy stayed in bed late, she served us our morning coffee.

> PAULA
> You despicable inhuman animal!

> RAFAEL
> Yes, an animal, if you like. But a Well-loved animal.

He holds up his hand to signal stop and his eyes begin to drift off again.

> RAFAEL
> No, it's nothing. Only James, and he's not talking about me... What were you saying?
> Yes, a despicable animal. Certainly. Why else would I be here?

He points to Paula.

RAFAEL
Your turn.

Paula cuts him a tense stare, then turns away shifting in her chair slightly.

PAULA
Well. I'm what some people up there, used to call "a damned bitch". Damned from the start. So it's no surprise, being here.

RAFAEL
Is that all you have to say?

PAULA
No. There's that affair with Jessica. A dead men's tale. With three corpses to it. He to start with; then she,
then I. So there's no one left, I've nothing to worry about; it was a clean sweep.

Paula has a distant look on her face.

PAULA
Only that room. I see it every now and then. Empty, with the doors locked... No, they've just un- locked them.

She strains her eyes reading.

PAULA
"To let". It's to let; there's a notice on the door. That's-too ridiculous!

Rafael strokes his chin.

    RAFAEL
    Three. Three deaths, you say?

    PAULA
    Three.

    RAFAEL
    One man and two women?

    PAULA
    Yes.

    RAFAEL
    Well, well.

Rafael pauses only to emphasise.

    RAFAEL
    Did he kill himself?

    PAULA
    Him? Nah, he didn't have the guts for all that. Still, he had every reason to; we'd led him a dogs life.
    As a matter of fact though, he was run over by a tram. A silly sort of end... I was living with them;
    he was my first-cousin.

    RAFAEL
    But was Jessica, fair?

    PAULA

Fair?

Paula glances over at Claudia.

PAULA
You know, I don't regret of thing; but still, I'm not exactly keen on telling the story to such a garbage person as yourself.

RAFAEL
That's alright, so you got sick of him?

Paula remains silent for a moment, then gradually begins to speak.

PAULA
All sorts of little things used to get on my nerves. Little things like the noise he used to make when he
was drinking-it was a kinda gurgle. Petty shit but annoying. He was rather pathetic really. Why are you smiling?

Rafael gives her a knowing smile.

RAFAEL
Because I, in any case, am not vulnerable.

Paula doesn't miss a beat.

PAULA
Don't be so sure... I crept inside her skin, she saw the world through my eyes. When she left him,
I had her in the palm of my hands. We shared a bed-sit flat on the other side of town.

Rafael try's to hide his anxiousness unsuccessfully.

RAFAEL
And then?

PAULA
And then the tram did it's job.

She smiles.

PAULA
I used to remind her everyday: "Yes, my pet. We killed him between us."

Sitting back.

PAULA
I'm rather cruel, really.

RAFAEL
So am I.

PAULA
No, you're not cruel. It's something else.

RAFAEL
What?

PAULA
I'll tell you later. When I say I'm cruel, I mean I can't get on without making other people suffer.
Like a hot piece of coal. But a hot coal in others' hearts. When I'm alone, I flicker out. For six months

I flamed away at her heart, until there was nothing but cinders left. One night she got up and turned on the gas
  as I slept, then she crept back into bed. Now you know.

RAFAEL
Well! well!

PAULA
What? What's on your mind?

RAFAEL
Nothing. Only that it's not a pretty story.

PAULA
Obviously. But what does that matter?

RAFAEL
As you say, of what does it matter?

He now turns to Claudia.

RAFAEL
Your turn. So, what have you done?

CLAUDIA
It's as I told you. I haven't any notion as to why I am here. I rack my brain, but it's no use.

Rafael rolls his eyes and presses her further.

RAFAEL
Right. Then we'll give you a hand. That fellow with the smashed face, who was he?

CLAUDIA
Who-who do you mean?

PAULA
You know quite well. The same man you were scared of seeing when you walked in.

CLAUDIA
Oh, him! A friend of mine.

RAFAEL
Why were you afraid of him?

CLAUDIA
That's my business, Mr Deschanel.

PAULA
Did he shoot himself on your account?

Claudia takes offence.

CLAUDIA
Of course not. How absurd you are!

RAFAEL
Then why should you have been so scared? He blew his brains out, didn't he? That's how he got his face smashed.

CLAUDIA
Don't. Please, don't go on.

RAFAEL

Because of you. Because of you.

PAULA
He shot himself because of you.

CLAUDIA
Leave me alone! It's-it's not fair, bullying me like this.

Claudia gets up from her seat.

CLAUDIA
I want to leave! I want to go!

Claudia makes a dash for the door and starts to shake at it.

RAFAEL
Go! If you can. Personally, I ask for nothing better. Unfortunately, the doors locked.

Claudia tries the door once more and then pushes the doorbell. The door bell doesn't make a sound.

Both Paula and Rafael start laughing.

She quickly turns on them with her back towards the door.

CLAUDIA
(stifled)
You're hateful, both of you.

PAULA
Hateful? Yes, that's the word. Now get on with it. That poor fellow who killed himself on your account-

you were his mistress, huh?

RAFAEL
Of course she was. And he wanted to have her to himself alone, isn't that so?

Paula is having fun.

PAULA
He danced the tango like a professional, but he was as poor as a church mouse-that's right, isn't it?

There's a silence in the room.

RAFAEL
Was he poor or not? Give a straight answer.

CLAUDIA
Yes he was poor.

RAFAEL
And you had your reputation to keep up. One day he came and implored you to run away with him, you laughed in his face.

Paula jumps up.

PAULA
That's it. You laughed at him. And so he killed himself.

CLAUDIA
And did you used to look at Jessica, that way?

PAULA

Yes.

There's a short silence and then Claudia bursts out laughing.

CLAUDIA
You've got it all wrong, you two.

With that she stiffens her shoulders, still leaning against the door she lifts her head to look them both dead on. The look on her face is confrontational as well as her tone of voice.

CLAUDIA
He wanted me to have a baby. So there!

RAFAEL
And you, didn't want one?

CLAUDIA
I most certainly did not. But the baby came, it was the worst luck... I went to Switzerland for five months.
No one knew anything. It was a girl. David was with me when she was born. It pleased him no- end,
having a daughter. It didn't please me!

RAFAEL
And then?

CLAUDIA
There was a balcony overlooking the lake. I brought a big stone. He could see what I was up too and kept on shouting:
"Claudia! For God's sake, don't!" I hated him. He saw it all. He was leaning over the balcony and he saw the rings
spreading on the water-

RAFAEL
Yes? Go on? And then?

CLAUDIA
That's all. I came back to Paris- and he did as he wished.

RAFAEL
You mean he blew his brains out?

CLAUDIA
It was absurd of him, really, my husband didn't suspect anything.

She pauses for a moment.

CLAUDIA
Oh, how I loathe you!
(She starts sobbing tearlessly.)

RAFAEL
Nothing doing. Tears don't flow in this place.

CLAUDIA
I'm a coward! A coward!

She takes another pause.

CLAUDIA
If you knew how I hate you!

Paula gets up and rushes to Claudia's side taking her into her arms.

PAULA

Poor child!

She then looks towards Rafael.

> PAULA
> So, the hearings are over now. But there's no need for you to look like the execution judge.

> RAFAEL
> Execution judge?

He glances around.

> RAFAEL
> I'd give a lot to be standing on the other-side of the glass in that particular role.

He adjusts his collar.

> RAFAEL
> How hot it is!

Without even thinking he takes off his jacket.

> RAFAEL
> Oh, sorry!

He starts putting it on again.

> CLAUDIA
> Oh, don't bother. You can stay in your shirt-sleeves. As things are-

RAFAEL
Just so.

He throws his jacket neatly into his seat.

RAFAEL
You mustn't be angry with me, Claudia.

CLAUDIA
I'm not angry with you.

PAULA
What about me? Are you angry with me?

A short silence.

CLAUDIA
Yes.

A shorter silence.

PAULA
Well, Mr Deschanel, now you have us in the nude alright. Do you understand things any better for that?

RAFAEL
I wonder. Yes, perhaps a trifle better.

His demeanour seems to soften slightly.

RAFAEL
And now suppose we start trying to help each other?

PAULA
I don't need help.

RAFAEL
Paula, they laid their snare damned cunningly-like a cobweb. If you make any movement,
 if you raise your hand to fan yourself, Claudia and I feel a little tug.

He wipes his forehead and tugs at his shirt-front as if the faint breeze will cool his body. He makes his plea.

RAFAEL
Alone, none of us can save himself or herself; we're linked inexplicably. So you need to make the choice.

The room is silent.

RAFAEL
Er, hello! What's happening?

PAULA
They've let it.

Paula has a distant look in her eyes.

PAULA
The windows are wide open, a man is sitting on my bed. My bed, if you please! I can't believe they've let it,
 let it! Roll up, roll up and step in and make yourself comfortable you brute! Ah, there's a woman there, too.
 She's going up to him, putting her hands on his shoulders...

Paula looks visibly upset as she observes something in the distance.

PAULA
Damn it, why don't they turn the lights on? It's getting dark. Now he's going to kiss her. But that's my room!

She strains her eyes.

PAULA
Pitch-dark now. I can't see anything, but I can hear them whispering, whispering.

A look of disgust comes over her.

PAULA
Is he go-ing to make love to her in my bed? What's that she's saying? ... That it's noon and the sun is shining? I must be going blind!

She leans forward squinting.

PAULA
Blacked out. I can't see or hear a thing. So I'm done with the earth, it seems. No more alibis for me!

She shudders.

PAULA
I feel so, so empty, cut-off, desiccated-really dead at last. All of me's here, in this room.

She blinks a couple times and rubs her eyes before looking around.

PAULA
What were you saying? Something about helping me, wasn't it?

RAFAEL
Yes.

PAULA
Helping me do what?

RAFAEL
To defeat their devilish tricks.

PAULA
And what do you expect me to do in return?

RAFAEL
To help me. It only needs a little effort, Paula; just a spark of human feeling.

Paula considers the proposition.

PAULA
Human feeling. That's beyond my range. I'm rotten to the core.

RAFAEL
And how about me?

He stops himself from biting.

RAFAEL
All the same, suppose we try?

PAULA
It's no use. I'm all dried up. I can't give and I can't receive. How can I help you? A dead twig, ready for the burning.

Paula casually sits back in her seat and stares at Claudia, who has her head placed in her hands.

PAULA
Jessica was fair, a natural blonde.

RAFAEL
You do realise that young woman's fated to be your torturer, don't you?

PAULA
Perhaps I've guessed it.

RAFAEL
It's through her that they'll get to you. I, of course, I'm different-aloof. I take no notice of her.
Suppose you had a try-

PAULA
Yes?

RAFAEL
It's a trap. They're watching you, to see if you'll fall into it.

Paula hasn't taken her eyes off Claudia.

PAULA
I know.

She looks directly at Rafael.

PAULA

And you're another trap. Do you think I haven't known your every word, even before you've said it?

And not to mention the nest of pitfalls and traps down here that we can't see. Everything here is a booby-trap.

But what do I care? I'm a pitfall, too. For her, obviously. And perhaps I'll catch her.

RAFAEL
You won't catch anything.

Rafael shakes his head.

RAFAEL
We're chasing each other, round and round in a vicious circle. Like the horses on a merry-go-round.

That's part of their plan, of course…

He tries again.

RAFAEL
Drop it, Paula. Open your hands and let go of everything. Or else you'll bring disaster upon all three of us.

PAULA
Do I like the sort of person who lets go? I know what's coming to me. I'm going to burn, and it lasts forever.

Yes, I know everything. But you think I'll let go?

She glances over to Claudia.

PAULA
I'll catch her, she'll see through my eyes, as Jessica saw that other man. What's the use of you trying to gain my sympathy?

I can assure you that I know everything, and I can't feel sorry even for myself.

She stands up defiantly.

PAULA
Yes, it's a trap! Don't I know it, and that I'm up to my neck in it.
There's nothing to be done about it, so if it suits their book, then so be it! So much the better for it!

Rafael grips hold of her shoulders.

RAFAEL
Well, I, anyhow, can feel sorry for you, too. Look at me, we're naked, naked right through, and I can see into your heart.
That's one link between us. Do you think I'd want to hurt you? I don't regret anything, I'm dried up, too.

He looks into Paula's eyes.

RAFAEL
...But for you, I can still feel pity.

Paula has let him keep his hands on her shoulders, shake them loose.

PAULA
Don't. I don't like being pawed. And keep your pity for yourself. Don't forget, Rafael, that they're traps for you,
too, in this room. All nicely set for you. You'd better watch your own interests...

Paula is in thought for a moment.

PAULA
But, if you will leave us in peace, this child and me, I will see that I won't do you any harm.

Rafael gazes at her for a moment, then shrugs his shoulders.

RAFAEL
Very well.

Claudia who has been silent and motionless suddenly raises her head from her hands.

CLAUDIA
Please, Rafael.

RAFAEL
What do you want of me?

Claudia stands up from her seat and walks over to him.

CLAUDIA
But you can still help, me.

He turns to face her.

RAFAEL
If you want help, apply to her.

Pointing to Paula, who has stood up and is now standing behind, Claudia. Rafael stands facing Claudia, he observes but doesn't speak.

CLAUDIA
I implore you, Rafael-you gave me your promise, didn't you?

Rafael is silent.

> CLAUDIA
> Help me quick, I don't want to be left alone. Verity's taken him to a nightclub.

Paula moves closer leaning into Claudia's ear from behind her but not touching her.

> PAULA
> Taking whom?

Claudia directs her answers to Rafael, as if he is the one speaking to her.

> CLAUDIA
> Peter... Oh, now they're dancing together.

> PAULA
> Whose Peter?

> CLAUDIA
> Such a silly boy. He called me his glancing stream-fancy that! He was terribly in love with me...
> She's persuaded him to come out with her?

Rafael continues to observe.

> PAULA
> Do you love him?

> CLAUDIA

They're sitting down now. She's bloody out of breath. What a fool the girl is insisting on dancing.

Although I've a good idea as to why... No, of course I don't love him; he's only 19, and I'm not a cradle snatcher!

PAULA
Then why bother about them? What difference can it make?

CLAUDIA
He, belonged, to me.

PAULA
Nothing on earth belongs to you anymore.

CLAUDIA
I tell you he was mine, all mine.

PAULA
Yes, he was yours-once... But now- try to make him hear, reach out and try to touch him.

Paula pauses momentarily to let her words sink in.

PAULA
Verity can touch him, she can talk to him as much as she likes. That's fact, isn't it? She can,
squeeze his hands, rub herself against him-

CLAUDIA
Yes, look! She's pressing her great fat chest against him, puffing and blowing in his face.

A smile appears on Paula's face.

CLAUDIA

But, my poor little lamb, can't you see how ridiculous she is? Why don't you laugh at her? Oh,
once I'd only have to but glance at them and she'd have slunk away. Is there really nothing left of me?

PAULA

Nothing whatsoever. Nothing of you is left on earth-not even a shadow.

Paula seems to be languishing in her role.

PAULA

All you own is here. Would you like a paper-knife? Or that ornament on the mantelpiece? That blue sofa's yours.
And I, my dear, am yours forever.

CLAUDIA

You mine! That's good! Well, which of you two would dare to call me their glancing stream, their crystal girl?
You know too much about me, you know I'm rotten through and through...

Paula is silent as Rafael continues to observe.

CLAUDIA

Peter dear, think of me, fix your thoughts on me, and save me. All the time you're thinking "my glancing stream,
my crystal girl," I'm only half here. I'm only half wicked, and half of me is down there with you, clean and bright
and crystal-clear as running water...

A furious look comes over Claudia's face.

> CLAUDIA
> Oh, just look at her face, all scarlet, like a tomato. No, it's absurd, we've laughed at her together, you and I,
> often and often... What's that tune?—I always loved it. Yes, the "St. LOUIS Blues"... All right, dance away, dance away.

Claudia starts moving her arm in time to an imaginary beat.

> CLAUDIA
> Rafael, I wish you could see her, you'd die of laughing. Only—she'll never know I see her. Yes, I see you, Verity,
> with your hair all anyhow, and you do look a dope, my dear. Oh, now you're treading on his toes. It's a scream!
> Hurry up! Quicker! Quicker! He's dragging her along, bundling her round and round—it's too ghastly!
> He always said I was so light, he loved to dance with me.

Claudia begins to dance as she speaks.

> CLAUDIA
> I tell you, Verity, I can see you. No, she doesn't care, she's dancing through my gaze. What's that?
> What's that you said? "Our poor dear Claudia"?

Claudia looks incredulously at her vision.

> CLAUDIA
> Oh, don't be such a bore! You didn't even shed a tear at the funeral... And she has the nerve to talk to him
> about her poor dear friend Claudia! How dare she discuss me with Peter? Now then, keep time.

She never could dance and talk at once.

Claudia slows her dancing.

CLAUDIA
Oh, what's that?! No, no. Don't tell him. Please, please don't tell him. You can keep him,
   do what you like with him, but please don't tell him about—that!

She suddenly stops dancing.

CLAUDIA
All right. You can have him now. Isn't it foul, Rafael? She's told him everything, about David,
   my trip to Switzerland, the baby..

Claudia now wears a look of shock resignation.

CLAUDIA (CONT'D)
"Poor Claudia wasn't exactly—" No, I wasn't exactly— True enough. He's looking grave, shaking his head,
   but he doesn't seem so very much surprised, not what one would expect.

Claudia resumes her dance at a toned down slower pace

CLAUDIA
Keep him, then—I won't haggle with you over his long eyelashes, his pretty girlish face. They're yours for the taking.
   His glancing stream, his crystal. Well, the crystal's shattered into bits. "Poor Claudia!" Dance, dance, dance.
   On with it. But do keep time. One, two. One, two. How I'd love to go down to earth for just a moment,

and dance with him again.

She continues to dance although losing momentum.

CLAUDIA
The music's growing fainter. They've turned down the lights, as they do for a slow dance. Why are they playing so softly?
Louder, please. I can't hear. It's so far away, so far away. I—I can't hear a sound.

She stops dancing.

CLAUDIA
All over. It's the end. The earth has left me.

She looks towards Rafael solemnly.

CLAUDIA
Don't turn from me—please. Take me in your arms.

From behind Claudia's back, Paula signals for Rafael to move away. Paula speaks commandingly.

PAULA
Now then, Rafael!

Rafael takes a step back and glances up at Claudia before pointing to Paula.

RAFAEL
It's to her you should say that.

Claudia walks up and clings to him.

CLAUDIA
Don't turn away. You're a man, aren't you and surely I'm not such a fright as all that! Everyone says I have lovely hair and,
after all a man killed himself on my account. You have to look at something, and there's nothings here to see
except the sofas and that awful ornament and the table.

She grips tighter to him pulling him close.

CLAUDIA
Surely I'm better to look at than a lot of stupid furniture. Listen! I've fallen from their hearts like a
little sparrow fallen from it's nest. So gather me up, dear, fold me into your heart-and you'll see how nice I can be.

Rafael tries to step away and free himself and Claudia pulls tighter. After a short struggle he frees himself.

RAFAEL
I tell you it's to that lady you should speak.

CLAUDIA
To her?! But she doesn't count, she's a woman.

PAULA
Oh, I don't count? Is that what you think? But, my poor little fallen nestling, you've been dealt a ring in my heart for ages,
though you didn't realise it. Don't be afraid; I'll keep looking at you forever and ever, without a flutter of my eyelids,
and you'll live in my gaze like a speck of dust in a sunbeam.

CLAUDIA

A sunbeam indeed! Don't talk such rubbish! You've tried that trick already, and you should know it doesn't work.

PAULA
Claudia! My glancing stream! My crystal!

CLAUDIA
Your crystal? It's grotesque. Do you think you can fool me with that sort of talk? Everyone knows by now
what I did to my baby. The crystal's shattered, but I don't care. I'm just a hollow dummy, all that's left of me
is the outside—but it's not for you.

PAULA
Come to me, Claudia. You shall be whatever you like: a glancing stream, a muddy stream. And deep down in my eyes
you'll see yourself just as you want to be.

CLAUDIA
Oh, leave me in peace. Either you haven't any eyes or they're full of dirt. Oh, damn it, isn't there anything I can do
to get rid of you? I've an idea.

Claudia spits in Paula's face.

CLAUDIA
There!

PAULA
Rafael, you shall pay for this.

There's a silence in the room. Rafael shrugs his shoulders and walks over to Claudia.

RAFAEL
So it's a man you need?

CLAUDIA
Not any man. You.

RAFAEL
Don't be such a bore. Any man would do your business. As I happen to be here, you want me. Right!

Rafael grips her by the shoulders.

RAFAEL
Mind you, I'm not your sort at all, really; I'm not a young nincompoop and I don't dance the tango.

CLAUDIA
I'll take you as you are. And perhaps I shall change you.

RAFAEL
I doubt it. I shan't pay much attention; I've other things to think about.

CLAUDIA
What things?

RAFAEL
They wouldn't interest you.

CLAUDIA
I'll sit on your sofa and wait for you to take some notice of me. I promise not to bother you at all.

Paula let's out a shrill laugh.

PAULA
That's right, fawn on him, like the silly bitch you are. Grovel and cringe! And he hasn't even good looks to commend him!

Claudia talks directly to Rafael.

CLAUDIA
Don't listen to her. She has no eyes, no ears. She's—nothing.

RAFAEL
I'll give you what I can. It doesn't amount to much. I shan't love you; I know you too well.

CLAUDIA
Do you want me, anyhow?

RAFAEL
Yes.

CLAUDIA
I ask no more.

RAFAEL
In that case—

Rafael proceeds to bend Claudia over a sofa.

PAULA
Claudia! Rafael! You must be going crazy. You're not alone. I'm here too.

RAFAEL
Of course-but what does that matter?

PAULA
Under my eyes? You couldn't- couldn't.

CLAUDIA
And why not? I've often undressed with my maid looking on.

Paula grabs hold of Rafael's arm.

PAULA
Leave her alone. Don't paw her with your dirty man's hands.

Rafael throws her back roughly.

RAFAEL
Take care. I'm no gentleman, and I'd have no compunction about striking a woman.

PAULA
But you promised me; you promised. I'm only asking you to keep your word.

RAFAEL
Why should I, considering you were the first to break our agreement?

Paula turns her back on him and retreats to the far side of the room.

PAULA

Very well, have it your own way. I'm the weaker party, one against two. But don't forget I'm here, and watching.

I won't take my eyes off you, Rafael; when you're kissing her, you'll feel them boring into you. Yes, have it your way,

make love and get it over. We're in hell; my turn will come.

Paula holds her corner silently watching the other two. Meanwhile Rafael has gone back to Claudia and has grasped her by her shoulders.

RAFAEL
Now then. Your lips. Give me your lips.

Rafael pauses, then bends to kiss her, stops then abruptly straightens up.

CLAUDIA
(indignantly)
Really...! Didn't I tell you not to pay any attention to her?

RAFAEL
No. You've got it wrong.

There's a short silence.

RAFAEL
It's James; he's back in the bunker. They've shut the windows; it must be winter down there. Six months since I—

Well, I warned you I'd be absent-minded sometimes, didn't I? They're shivering, they've kept their coats on.

Funny they should feel the cold like that, when I'm feeling so hot. Ah, this time he's talking about me.

CLAUDIA
Is it going to last long?

Rafael doesn't answer.

> CLAUDIA
> You might at least tell me what he's saying.

> RAFAEL
> Nothing. Nothing worth repeating. He's a swine, that's all!

Rafael listens on attentively.

> RAFAEL
> A god-damned bloody swine.

He turns back towards Claudia.

> RAFAEL
> Let's come back to—to ourselves. Are you going to love me?

She smiles.

> CLAUDIA
> I wonder now!

> RAFAEL
> Will you trust me?

> CLAUDIA
> What a quaint thing to ask! Considering you'll be under my eyes all the time, and I don't think I've much
> to fear from Paula, so far as you're concerned.

> RAFAEL

Obviously.

Rafael pauses and takes his hands off her shoulders.

RAFAEL
I was thinking of another kind of trust.

Rafael is listening to something.

RAFAEL
Talk away, talk away, you swine. I'm not there to defend myself.

He looks at Claudia.

RAFAEL
Claudia, you must give me your trust.

CLAUDIA
Oh, what a nuisance you are! I'm giving you my mouth, my arms, my whole body— and everything could be so simple...
My trust! I haven't any to give, I'm afraid, and you're making me terribly embarrassed. You must have something
pretty ghastly on your conscience to make such a fuss about my trusting you.

RAFAEL
They shot me.

CLAUDIA
I know. Because you refused to give in. Well, why should you?

RAFAEL
It wasn't exactly like that.

Rafael speaks in a far-away distant voice.

RAFAEL
I must say he talks well, he makes out a good case against me, but he never says what he would have done instead.
Should I have gone to the treasury and said: "We've stumbled onto a veritable windfall; but I'm going to hold onto to it,
so we don't end up giving it away to the very people we're fighting against?" A mugs game; they'd have promptly locked me up.
But I wanted to show them my colours, my true colours, do you understand? I wasn't going to be silenced.

CLAUDIA
Of course not, you're a fighter.

He looks at Claudia cautiously.

RAFAEL
So I-I took a plane.

CLAUDIA
Where were you trying to go?

RAFAEL
To Italy. I meant to launch a new political party, one more aligned to the will of the people. But I had to lay low,
how was I to know it was a civil service pension fund? Before I knew it, it was out of my control-I couldn't make it right.
The irony being; the opposition caught up to me before the authorities... They made light work of me.

There's a short silence.

RAFAEL
Well, why don't you speak?

CLAUDIA
What could I say? You acted quite rightly, if you weren't ready to fight.

Rafael makes a worried looking gesture.

CLAUDIA
But, darling, how on earth can I guess what you want me to answer?

PAULA
Can't you guess? Well, I can. He wants you to tell him that he never bolted away like the thieving cowardly rat
that he really is. For "bolt" he did and that's what's biting him.

RAFAEL
"Bolted" "went away", we won't quarrel over words.

CLAUDIA
But you had to run away. If you'd stayed they'd have sent you to jail, wouldn't they?

RAFAEL
Of course.

He's silent for a moment.

RAFAEL
Well, Claudia, am I a coward?

CLAUDIA
How can I say? Don't be so unreasonable, darling. I can't put myself in your skin. You must decide that for yourself.

RAFAEL
(wearily) I can't decide.

CLAUDIA
Anyhow, you must remember. You must have had reasons for acting as you did.

RAFAEL
I had.

CLAUDIA
Well?

RAFAEL
(Pondering)
But were they the real reasons?

CLAUDIA
You've a twisted mind, that's your trouble. Plaguing yourself over such trifles!

RAFAEL
I'd thought it all out, and I wanted to make a stand. But was that my real motive?

PAULA
Exactly. That's the question. Was that your real motive? No doubt you argued it out with yourself,

you weighed the pros and cons, you found good reasons for what you did. But fear and hatred and all the dirty

little instincts one keeps dark—they're motives too. So carry on, Mr. Deschanel, and try to be honest

with yourself—for once.

RAFAEL
Do I need you to tell me that? Day and night I paced my one-roomed bungalow, from the window to the door,

from the door to the window.

He begins to pace back and forth.

RAFAEL
I pried into my heart, I sleuthed myself like a detective. By the end of it I felt as if I'd given my whole life to introspection.

But always I harked back to the one thing certain—that I had acted as I did, I'd taken that plane

and fled to the mountains. But why? Why?

Finally I thought: My death will settle it. If I face death courageously, I'll prove I am no coward.

Paula is on cue.

PAULA
And how did you face death?

RAFAEL
Miserably. Rottenly. With defecation.

Paula bursts out into laughter.

RAFAEL

Oh, it was only a physical lapse—that might happen to anyone; I'm not ashamed of it. Only everything's
been left in suspense forever.

He looks over to Claudia.

RAFAEL
Come here, Claudia. Look at me. I want to feel someone looking at me while they're talking about me on earth...
I like green eyes.

PAULA
Green eyes! Just listen to him! And you, Claudia, do you like cowards?

CLAUDIA
If you knew how little I care! Coward or hero, it's all one—provided he kisses well.

RAFAEL
There they are, slumped in their chairs, sucking at their cigars. Bored they look. Half-asleep. They're thinking:
"Rafael's a coward." But only vaguely, dreamily. One's got to think of something. "That chap Rafael was a coward."
That's what they've decided, those dear friends of mine. In six months' time they'll be saying:
"Cowardly as that skunk Rafael." You're lucky, you two; no one on earth is giving you another thought.
But I—I'm long in dying.

PAULA
What about your wife, Rafael?

RAFAEL
Oh, didn't I tell you? She's dead.

PAULA
Dead?

RAFAEL
Yes, she died just now. About two months ago.

PAULA
Of grief?

RAFAEL
What else should she die of? So all is for the best, you see; it's the end of segregation, beginning of integration,
    my wife's dead, and I've carved out my place in history.

He gives out a choking sob and passes his hand over his face. Claudia catches his arm.

CLAUDIA
My poor darling! Look at me. Please look. Touch me. Touch me.

Claudia takes Rafael's hand and puts it on her neck.

CLAUDIA
There! Keep your hand there.

Rafael makes a worried look.

CLAUDIA
No, don't move. Why trouble what those men are thinking? They'll die off one by one. Forget them.

There's only me, now.

RAFAEL
But they won't forget me, not they! They'll die, but others will come after them to carry on the legend.
I've left my fate in their hands.

CLAUDIA
You think too much, that's your trouble.

RAFAEL
What else is there to do now? I was a man of action once... Oh, if only I could be with them again, for just one day—
I'd fling their lie in their teeth. But I'm locked out; they're passing judgment on my life without troubling about me,
and they're right, because I'm dead. Dead and done with.

He laughs out loud.

RAFAEL
A laughing stock.

Silence in the room. Claudia speaks gently.

CLAUDIA
Rafael.

RAFAEL
Still there? Now listen! I want you to do me a service. No, don't shrink away. I know it must seem strange to you,
having someone asking you for help; you're not used to that. But if you'll make the effort, if you'll only will it hard enough,

I dare say we can really love each other. Look at it this way. A thousand of them are proclaiming I'm a coward;

but what do numbers matter? If there's someone, just one person, to say quite positively I did not run away,

that I'm not the sort who runs away, that I'm brave and decent and the rest of it—well,

that one person's faith would save me. Will you have that faith in me?

Then I shall love you and cherish you for ever. Claudia—will you?

Claudia finds this hilarious.

CLAUDIA
(laughing)
Oh, you dear silly man, do you think I could love a coward?

RAFAEL
But just now you said—

CLAUDIA
I was only teasing you. I like men, my dear, who're real men, with tough skin and strong hands.

You haven't a coward's chin, or a coward's mouth, or a coward's voice, or a coward's hair.

And it's for your mouth, your hair, your voice, I love you.

RAFAEL
Do you mean this? Really mean it?

CLAUDIA
Shall I swear it?

RAFAEL
Then I snap my fingers at them all, those above and those in here.

Claudia, we shall climb out of hell.

Paula gives a shrill laugh at this. He breaks off and stares at her

RAFAEL
What's that?

PAULA
(still laughing)
But she doesn't mean a word of what she says. How can you be such a simpleton? "Claudia, am I a coward?"
As if she cared a damn either way.

CLAUDIA
Paula, how dare you?

She turns again to Rafael.

CLAUDIA
Don't listen to her. If you want me to have faith in you, you must begin by trust-ing me.

PAULA
That's right! That's right! Trust away! She wants a man—that far you can trust her—she want's a man's arm
round her waist, a man's smell, a man's eyes glowing with desire.
And that's all she wants. She'd assure you you were God Almighty if she thought it would give you pleasure.

RAFAEL
Claudia, is this true? Answer me. Is it true?

CLAUDIA

What do you expect me to say? Don't you realise how maddening it is to have to answer questions one
can't make head or tail of?

Claudia stamps her foot.

CLAUDIA
You do make things difficult... Anyhow, I'd love you just the same, even if you were a coward. Isn't that enough?

There's a short silence in the room. Rafael addresses both women.

RAFAEL
You disgust me, both of you.

He walks towards the door.

CLAUDIA
What are you up to?

RAFAEL
I'm going.

Paula quicklime interjects.

PAULA
You won't get far. The door is locked.

RAFAEL
I'll make them open it.

He presses the bell-push. The bell does not ring.

CLAUDIA
Please! Please!

PAULA
Don't worry, my pet. The bell doesn't work.

RAFAEL
I tell you they shall open.

He begins to drum on the door.

RAFAEL
I can't endure it any longer, I'm through with you both.

Claudia runs to the door; he pushes her away.

RAFAEL
Go away. You're even fouler than she. I won't let myself get bogged in your eyes. You're soft and slimy. Ugh!

He bangs at the door again.

RAFAEL
Like an octopus. Like a quagmire.

CLAUDIA
I beg you, oh, I beg you not to leave me. I'll promise not to speak again, I won't trouble you in any way—but don't go!
I daren't be left alone with Paula, now she's shown her claws.

RAFAEL
Look after yourself. I never asked you to come here.

CLAUDIA
Oh, how mean you are! Yes, it's quite true you're a coward.

Paula approaches Claudia.

PAULA
Well, my little sparrow fallen from the nest, I hope you're satisfied now. You spat in my face—playing up to him,
of course—and we had a fight on his account. But he's going, and a good riddance it will be. We two women
will have the place to ourselves.

CLAUDIA
You won't gain anything. If that door opens, I'm going, too.

PAULA
Where?

CLAUDIA
I don't care where. As far from you as I can.

Rafael has been banging on the door continuously while they talk.

RAFAEL
Open the door! Open, blast you! I'll endure anything, your red-hot tongs and molten lead, your racks and prongs
and whips and chains-- all your fiendish gadgets, everything that burns and flays and tears—
I'll put up with any torture you impose.

He stops beating the door in order to catch his breath.

RAFAEL

Anything, anything would be better than this agony of mind, this creeping pain that gnaws and fumbles
and caresses one and never hurts quite enough.

He grips the door-knob hard and begins to rattling it.

>RAFAEL
>Now will you open?!

The door suddenly flies open with a jerk, he narrowly avoids falling over.

>RAFAEL
>Ah!

There's a long silence in the room as Rafael stands by the now open door.

>PAULA
>Well, Rafael? You're free to go.

Rafael speaks reflectivity.

>RAFAEL
>Now I wonder why that door opened.

>PAULA
>What are you waiting for? Hurry up and go!

>RAFAEL
>I shall not go.

>PAULA
>And you, Claudia?

Claudia does not move or say a word. Paula bursts out laughing.

> PAULA
> So what? Which shall it be? Which of the three of us will leave? The barrier's down, why are we waiting?.. But what a situation!
> It's a scream! We're—inseparables!

Claudia springs her from behind.

> CLAUDIA
> Inseparables? Rafael, come and lend a hand. Quickly. We'll push her out and slam the door on her. That'll teach her a lesson.

Paula struggles with Claudia.

> PAULA
> Claudia! I beg you, let me stay. I won't go, I won't go! Not into the passage.

> RAFAEL
> Let go of her.

> CLAUDIA
> You're crazy. She hates you.

> RAFAEL
> It's because of her I'm staying here.

Claudia releases Paula and stares dumbfoundedly at Rafael.

> PAULA
> Because of me?

She thinks about this for a moment.

PAULA
All right, shut the door. It's ten times hotter here since it opened.

Rafael goes to the door and shuts it.

PAULA
Because of me, you said?

RAFAEL
Yes. You, anyhow, know what it means to be a coward.

PAULA
Yes, I know.

RAFAEL
And you know what wickedness is, and shame, and fear. There were days when you peered into yourself,
into the secret places of your heart, and what you saw there made you faint with horror. And then, next day,
you didn't I know what to make of it, you couldn't interpret the horror you had glimpsed the day before. Yes,
you know what evil costs. And when you say I'm a coward, you know from experience what that means. Is that so?

PAULA
Yes.

RAFAEL
SO it's you whom I have to convince; you are of my kind. Did you suppose I meant to go? No, I couldn't leave you here,

gloating over my defeat, with all those thoughts about me running in your head.

PAULA
Do you really wish to convince me?

RAFAEL
That's the one and only thing I wish for now. I can't hear them any longer, you know. Probably that means
they're through with me. For good and all. The curtain's down, nothing of me is left on earth—
not even the name of coward. So, Paula, we're alone. Only you two remain to give a thought to me. She—she doesn't count.
It's you who matter; you who hate me. If you'll have faith in me I'm saved.

PAULA
It won't be easy. Have a look at me. I'm a hard-headed woman.

RAFAEL
I'll give you all the time that's needed.

PAULA
Yes, we've lots of time in hand. All time.

Rafael rests his hands on her shoulders.

RAFAEL
Listen! Each man has an aim in life, a leading motive; that's so, isn't it? Well, I didn't give a damn for wealth, or for love.
I aimed at being a real man. A 'tough guy', as they say. I staked everything on the same horse... Can one possibly be a coward

when one's deliberately courted danger at every turn? And can one judge a life by a single action?

PAULA

Why not? For thirty years you dreamt you were a hero, and condoned a thousand petty lapses—because a hero,
of course, can do no wrong. An easy method, obviously. Then a day came when you were up against it, the red light of real danger
—and you took the plane to Italy; leaving everyone who trusted you worse off for it.

RAFAEL

I "dreamt," you say. It was no dream. When I chose the hardest path, I made my choice deliberately. A man is
what he wills himself to be.

PAULA

Prove it. Prove it was no dream. It's what one does, and nothing else, that shows the stuff one's made of.

RAFAEL

I died too soon. I wasn't allowed time to—to do my deeds.

PAULA

One always dies too soon—or too late. And yet one's whole life is complete at that moment, with a line drawn
neatly under it, ready for the summing up. You are—your life, and nothing else.

RAFAEL

What a poisonous woman you are! With an answer for everything.

PAULA

Now then, bigot! Don't lose heart. It shouldn't be so hard, convincing me. Pull yourself together, man, rake up some arguments.

Rafael shrugs his shoulders.

PAULA
Ah, wasn't I right when I said you were vulnerable? Now you're going to pay the price, and what a price!
You're a coward, Rafael, because I wish it. I wish it—do you hear?—I wish it. And yet, just look at me,
see how weak I am, a mere breath on the air, a hard gaze observing you, a formless thought that thinks you.

He begins to walk over to her, opening his hands.

PAULA
Ah, they're open now, those big hands, those coarse, man's hands! But what do you hope to do? You can't throttle
thoughts with hands. So you've no choice, you must convince me, and you're at my mercy.

CLAUDIA
Rafael!

RAFAEL
What?

CLAUDIA
Avenge yourself!

RAFAEL
How?

CLAUDIA
Kiss me, darling—then you'll hear her squeal.

RAFAEL
That's true, Paula. I'm at your mercy, but you're at mine as well.

He bends over Claudia. Paula gives out a little cry.

PAULA
Oh, you coward, you weakling, running to women to console you!

CLAUDIA
That's right, Paula. Squeal away.

PAULA
What a lovely pair you make! If you could see his big paw splayed out on your back, rucking up your skin
and creasing the silk. Be careful, though! He's sweating, his hand's gonna leave a blue stain on your dress.

CLAUDIA
Squeal away, Paula, squeal away!... Hug me tight, darling; tighter still—that'll finish her off, and a good thing too!

PAULA
Yes, Rafael, she's right. Carry on with it, press her to you till you feel your bodies melting into each other;
a lump of warm, throbbing flesh... Love's a grand solace, isn't it, my friend? Deep and dark as sleep.
But I'll see you don't sleep.

CLAUDIA

Don't listen to her. Press your lips to my mouth. Oh, I'm yours, yours, yours.

PAULA
Well, what are you waiting for? Do as you're told. What a lovely scene: coward Rafael holding baby-killer

Claudia in his manly arms! Make your stakes, everyone. Will coward Rafael kiss the lady, or won't he dare?

What's the betting? I'm watching you, everybody's watching, I'm a crowd all by myself. Do you hear the crowd?

Do you hear them muttering, Rafael? Mumbling and muttering. "Coward! Coward! Coward! Coward!"

—that's what they're saying... It's no use trying to escape, I'll never let you go.

What do you hope to get from her silly lips? Forgetfulness? But I shan't forget you, not I!

"It's I you must convince." So come to me. I'm waiting. Come along, now...

Look how obedient he is, like a well- trained dog who comes when his mistress calls. You can't hold him, and you never will.

RAFAEL
Will night never come?

PAULA
Never.

RAFAEL
You will always see me?

PAULA
Always.

Rafael moves away from Claudia and take some steps across the room. He goes to the bronze ornament.

RAFAEL
This bronze.

He begins to stroke it thoughtfully.

RAFAEL
Yes, now's the moment; I'm looking at this thing on the mantelpiece, and I understand that I'm in hell.
I tell you, everything's been thought out beforehand. They knew I'd stand at the fire-place stroking this thing of bronze,
with all those eyes intent on me.
Devouring me.

He swings round abruptly.

RAFAEL
What? Only two of you? I thought there were more; many more.

He begins to laugh.

RAFAEL
So this is hell. I'd never have believed it. You remember all we were told about the torture- chambers,
the fire and brimstone, the "burning marl." Old wives' tales! There's no need for red-hot pokers.
Hell is—other people!

CLAUDIA
My darling! Please—

Claudia throws herself at him and he thrusts her away.

RAFAEL
No, let me be. She is between us. I cannot love you when she's watching.

CLAUDIA
Right! In that case, I'll stop her watching.

Claudia picks up the paper-knife from the table, then rushes Paula stabbing her several times.

PAULA
(struggling and laughing) But, you crazy creature, what do you think you're doing? You know quite well I'm dead.

CLAUDIA
Dead?

Claudia drops the knife. There's a moment of silence before Paula picks up the knife and starts jabbing herself with it regretfully.

PAULA
Dead! Dead! Dead! Knives, poison, ropes—all useless. It has happened already, do you understand?
Once and for all. So here we are, forever.

Paula then bursts out laughing.

CLAUDIA
(with a burst of laughter) Forever. My God, how funny!
Forever.

Rafael looks at the two women, and joins in the laughter.

>RAFAEL
>For ever, and ever, and ever.

They slump onto their respective sofas. A long silence. Their laughter dies away and they gaze at each other.

>RAFAEL
>Well, well, let's get on with it...

THE END

www.ingramcontent.com/pod-product-compliance
Lightning Source LLC
LaVergne TN
LVHW072021060526
838200LV00009B/227